Tiny Travellers
In
HONG KONG

Design and illustrations by Ann Beatty
Edited by Ken Keobke

ISBN 962-85029-5-6
Copyright © 1995 by Precocious Press Ltd
Published in association with Maplewood Press

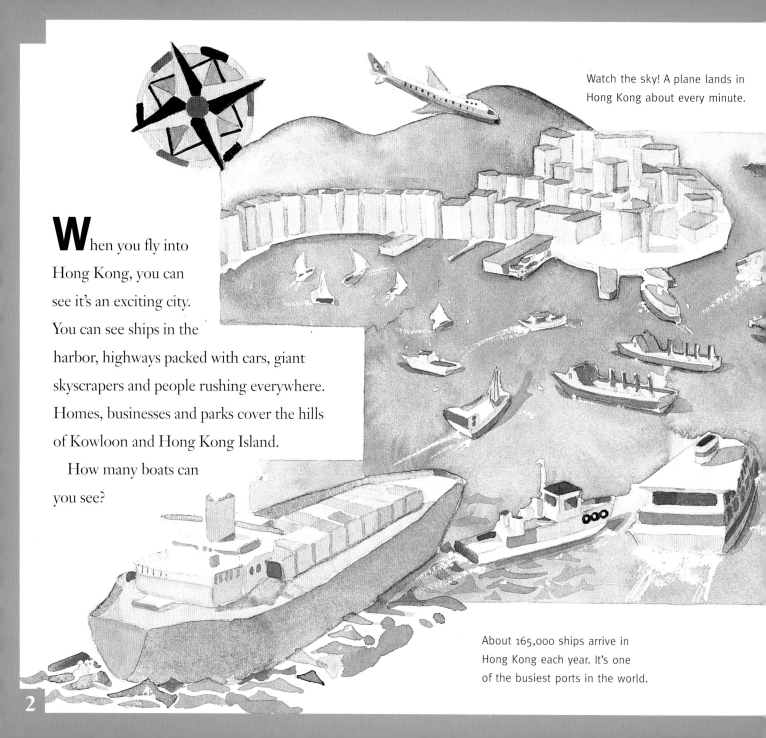

Watch the sky! A plane lands in Hong Kong about every minute.

When you fly into Hong Kong, you can see it's an exciting city. You can see ships in the harbor, highways packed with cars, giant skyscrapers and people rushing everywhere. Homes, businesses and parks cover the hills of Kowloon and Hong Kong Island.

How many boats can you see?

About 165,000 ships arrive in Hong Kong each year. It's one of the busiest ports in the world.

In Hong Kong, you can ride on top of the old-fashioned trams and double-decker buses.

Great Britain won Hong Kong Island in a war with China in 1841. Later, the colony expanded to include parts of the nearby mainland, called Kowloon and the New Territories. Britain agreed to return the colony to China on July 1, 1997.

From Central you can take a ferry to the Portuguese colony of Macau.

Hong Kong's 6.2 million people live together in a very small place. Most Hong Kong people are Chinese. They speak a language called Cantonese. A few common Cantonese words are "Mm goy," which means "Thank you," and "Jo san," which means "Good morning."

Look for these signs:

RESTAURANT   EXIT   PERSON

Many Hong Kong people live in tall apartment blocks. Sometimes they dry their clothes on bamboo poles.

In Hong Kong, people love to talk on mobile phones. There are about 350,000 mobile phones in Hong Kong, one for every 17 people.

4

Visit these Chinese neighborhoods:
Causeway Bay and Western District on Hong
Kong Island, and Mong Kok in Kowloon.

You can buy a stone chop
to stamp your name in
Chinese or English.

Hong Kong shoppers enjoy the outdoor markets. Here they can buy clothes, toys, watches and fresh food.

Hawkers are people whose whole store is just a cart. They stop on street corners to sell breakfast, lunch and dinner. Some hawkers sell shirts, clocks and CDs.

How many people are shopping here?

Legends say dragons travel over Hong Kong Island each night. The opening in the ground floor of the Hongkong Bank building allows the dragons to pass through.

The Dragon is one of the most popular symbols in Chinese culture. Ancient Chinese believed dragons lived in the hills of Kowloon. In fact, *Kowloon* is the Chinese word "Nine Dragons." Each Chinese year has a different animal: The Snake, Horse, Sheep, Monkey, Rooster, Dog, Pig, Rat, Ox/Cow, Tiger, Rabbit and Dragon. Which animal are you? Ask your Chinese friends.

Try to see a Lion Dance at Chinese New Year or during any other Chinese holiday.

The Chinese invented firecrackers and fireworks. Each New Year is celebrated with a great fireworks display over the harbor.

The most important festival in Hong Kong is Chinese New Year. Married people give children red envelopes filled with money. These envelopes are called *Lai See*. Remember to greet people with "Kung Hei Fat Choy,"

which means "May you prosper in the New Year."

During Chinese New Year, you can see small orange trees called kumquats in shops, offices and homes.

The 2,000-year-old Dragon Boat Festival is held each spring. Teams from around the world come to race.

Late night picnics, munching mooncakes and lighting paper lanterns are highlights of the Mid-Autumn Festival. How many lanterns can you see?

Families gather in Victoria Park to light candles and play with colorful lanterns beneath the first moon of the New Year.

Feng Shui means "Earth and Water." Experts use this mystical compass to decide on a building's lucky directions.

Chinese believe you will have good luck, or *feng shui*, if your house or office is properly designed and decorated. Fish tanks bring good luck, so there are many fish tanks in Hong Kong. The best *feng shui* is to have a great mountain behind you and the ocean in front of you.

According to Feng Shui, brightly colored fish, especially carp and goldfish, bring good luck.

Hong Kong's main business area is called Central. It is also where you will find Hong Kong Park.

Visit the giant Aviary, and walk across suspended bridges. Look for each of the 600 exotic birds, including fairy bluebirds and straw crowned bulbuls. How many birds can you count?

Flamingoes get their color from eating pink shrimp.

The pelican's beak has a huge pouch that scoops up fish. It's just like a built-in net.

The two-dollar coin has an engraving of Hong Kong's flower, the Bauhinia. What's on the other side?

The Hong Kong Zoological and Botanical Gardens are nearby. Here you can see huge Bornean orangutans, lion-tailed macaques, Goodfellow's tree kangaroos and chimpanzees. In the morning, people come here to practice T'ai Chi, a slow and graceful form of martial arts.

Ride the Peak Tram up Hong Kong Island's highest mountain. Walk around The Peak and see all of Hong Kong.

The Bird Market sells birds, bird cages and bird food, including live worms! Singing birds are the most expensive.

Across the harbor from Central is the tourist district of Tsim Sha Tsui — just say "T.S.T." Thousands of tiny stores are lit by bright neon lights. But none of the lights flash. This is because people worried that flashing lights would confuse the sailors. T.S.T. has the Cultural Center and museums for art, space, science and history.

What's your favorite museum?

The Clock Tower is in front of the Cultural Center. It was part of the Railway station for the train to China. It was built in 1916.

The Hong Kong Space Museum has displays on the planets, stars and space travel. It also has an Omnimax cinema.

The best way to get to Tsim Sha Tsui is the Star Ferry. It has been taking people across the harbor since 1868. It only takes eight minutes. Sit near the back of the ferry so you can look at the skyscrapers of Central and The Peak.

Hong Kong has 235 islands. Ferries from Central take you to the three largest islands: Lantau, Lamma and Cheung Chau. These islands have great hiking trails, but wear a hat and carry water. It can be hot!

The Chinese fishing villages have seafood restaurants. Everything is very fresh. In fact, it's still alive! Just point at the fish you want to eat.

LANTAU ISLAND

CHEUNG CHAU

Visit the Pirate's Cave on Cheung Chau.

In some temples, coiled incense hangs from the ceiling. It's burned in memory of the dead.

HONG KONG ISLAND

LAMMA ISLAND

Build sandcastles on the beach.

The largest island in Hong Kong is Lantau, home of Hong Kong's new airport. On top of one mountain you can see a huge bronze Buddha. The statue is 26 meters tall, about as high as a six-story building.

Around the statue is Po Lin Monastery, the main center for Buddhism in Hong Kong. How many islands can you count?

See these shows at Ocean Park: *Ocean Theater* (tricks by marine animals); *Emperor Theater* (displays of Chinese culture); *High diving pool*; *Bird Theater* and *Kid's World Theater*.

Ocean Park is a fun place to learn about the ocean and enjoy the rides. Imagine a tank, three-stories high, full of colorful fish! It also has a pool of dangerous sharks. Nearby, seals play in a make-believe ocean. You can even ride in a cable car to get to the exhibits.

Take a trip along the *Dinosaur Discovery Trail* or see all of Hong Kong from *Ocean Park Tower*.

Ocean Park has lots of fun rides, like the huge rollercoaster called *The Dragon*, or the water ride called *The Raging River*.

In the *Atoll Reef*, you can see the fish and animals that live around a coral reef.

Next to Ocean Park, you'll find Water World. It's a huge tangle of swimming pools and waterslides; just the thing to cool you down during hot Hong Kong summers. You can spend hours trying the twisting, turning waterslides. There are deep pools and shallow pools. It's fun whether or not you can swim.

Hong Kong is a modern city but you can still see small family farms where vegetables are grown. On some farms, water buffalo are still used to pull ploughs.

North of Kowloon are the New Territories. Almost half the people in Hong Kong live here. It also has most of Hong Kong's farmland. There are lots of hiking trails. Sai Kung Country Park is a great place for a family picnic.

Women wear straw hats with cloth around the edges to keep the sun off. These are called *Hakka* cool hats.

Look for the noodle maker, a traditional Chinese occupation that goes back hundreds of years.

Shake the sticks until one fortune stick falls out.

NATURE TRAIL

Visit the Sung Dynasty Village to see how the Chinese people lived a thousand years ago. Actors dress in costumes from that time and show you the traditional crafts and food.

How many ducks are swimming?

Hiking is very popular on the weekends. There are 21 country parks for you to explore.

Visit a floating restaurant in Aberdeen. Once, most of the people in Aberdeen lived on little boats called *sampans*.

The most popular part of Chinese culture is Chinese food. Hong Kong has great Chinese restaurants that will serve you a *Dim Sum* lunch where you pick each small dish from a cart. Many restaurants are bright and noisy. Children are always welcome!

What's your favorite food?

How to hold chopsticks:

Place one stick between your thumb and first finger. Hold the other with the tips of the thumb, first and second fingers.

Dried, flattened duck is one Cantonese specialty. Another is spicy chickens' feet.

There are so many things to do in Hong Kong, you may not be able to squeeze them all in during one visit. But even if you only see a few of these sights, you'll always remember Hong Kong as an exciting and fun place. Come back soon!

PARENTS' GUIDE TO HONG KONG

This book is designed to show children the educational and fun sides of Hong Kong. Here are attractions with prices (as of Nov 1995) as well as transportation notes. All directions assume you are starting from Central.

Prices are in Hong Kong dollars (HK$7.75 is about US$1). *MTR* means *Mass Transit Railway*, the subway or underground system.

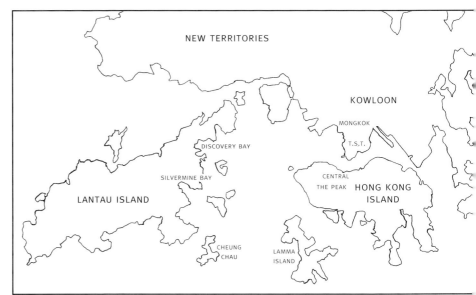

CLIMATE:

Hong Kong's climate is subtropical from May to Sept so dress lightly and bring hats. If you plan to hike, avoid the hottest part of the day and carry plenty of water. Winter can be damp and chilly. ● Typhoons occur during the summer and are announced on radio and TV. The signals are also posted around town. Signals reflect the typhoon's proximity to Hong Kong. Don't plan long trips during a Number 3. The next signal, Number 8, closes down Hong Kong; ferries soon stop and stores close. Stay inside! At Signal 8 or 10 (a direct hit), the airport closes. Taxi drivers sometimes hike fares dramatically (and illegally) during typhoons.

SAFETY TIPS:

Traffic moves quickly in Hong Kong and cars travel on the left hand side of the road; always look both ways before crossing. ● Tap water is generally safe for drinking; bottled water is also widely available. ● Chinese adore babies and small children so waitresses and strangers may approach them or pick them up. If this makes you uncomfortable, politely say so. ● Sadly, many Hong Kong beaches are polluted and there may be dangerous sharp objects in the sand. Watch your children and ensure they wear runners or waterproof shoes. ● Hong Kong's crime rate is lower than most cities, but beware of pickpockets and deals that are too good to be true. ● Wash fruit and vegetables.

TELEPHONE NUMBERS:

Emergencies (Police, fire, ambulances) 999
Police hotline (and taxi complaints) 2866 6166

Free Ambulance Service

Hong Kong Island
2576 6555

Kowloon/New Territories
2713 5555

Hospital 24-hour casualty wards:

Queen Mary Hospital,
Hong Kong Island   2855 4111

Queen Elizabeth Hospital,
Kowloon   2710 2111

Prince of Wales Hospital, Sha Tin,
New Territories   2636 2211

Ocean Park/Waterworld
2555 3554

Ferry times for Outlying Islands
2542 3082

Tourist Information
2807 6177

ATTRACTIONS:

Take the MTR to the Chinese Neighborhoods (Pg 4-5): Mong Kok or Causeway Bay stations for those areas and Sheung Wan station for Western District.

Festivals (Pg 6-8): Check with Tourist Information for exact dates. Chinese New Year is around February and fireworks are best seen from the harbor walk in Tsim Sha Tsui. This is also the best place to watch the Dragon Boat Races, held around June. Mid-Autumn Festival, held in September or October is best seen in Victoria Park (near the Causeway Bay MTR station) or on The Peak (take the Peak Tram).

Aviary in Hong Kong Park (Pg 10): Go by MTR to Admiralty station, then follow the signs through Pacific Place to escalators which go right to HK Park. The Aviary is open 9 a.m.-5 p.m. (9-4:30 Oct 1-Jan 31), seven days a week. Admission is free.

Hong Kong Zoological and Botanical Gardens (Pg 11): From Hong Kong Park, cross Cotton Tree Drive and Garden Drive. Open 6:30 a.m.-7p.m., everyday. Free.

The Peak Tram (Pg 11): Uphill from Citibank Plaza and open 10 a.m.-8p.m., seven days a week. Tickets are $14 for adults or $21 return; $4 for Children or $7 return. The 3.5 kilometer Peak walking trail is suitable for strollers and has spectacular views and a playground.

Bird Market (Pg 12): Take the MTR to Mong Kok station. Use the north exit. Open 10 a.m.-6 p.m.

Star Ferry (Pg 13): $1.70 for the upper deck, and $1.40 for the lower deck. The Central-Tsim Sha Tsui ferry runs every 5-15 minutes from 6:30 a.m. to 11:30 p.m.

Hong Kong Museum of Art (Pg 12): Cultural Centre complex. Take the Star Ferry to Tsim Sha Tsui and walk to the Cultural Centre. Open everyday except Thursdays, 10 a.m.-6 p.m. and 1-6 p.m. Sundays. Phone for holiday hours. Admission $10 for adults, $5 for children.

Hong Kong Space Museum (Pg 13): The ball-shaped museum is a 5 minute walk past the Cultural Centre. Open Mon, Wed-Fri 1-9 p.m., Sat-Sun and holidays 10 a.m.-9 p.m.; closed Tuesdays and some holidays. Admission $10 for adults, $5 for children; includes the Planetarium. Space Theatre admission $26 for adults, $13 for children. Children under 3 are not admitted to the theater.

Hong Kong Museum of History (Pg 12): Take the MTR to Tsim Sha Tsui and exit to Kowloon Park. Open everyday 10 a.m.-6 p.m and 1-6 p.m. Sundays. Phone for holiday hours. Admission $10 for adults, $5 for children.

Hong Kong Science Museum (Pg 12): Science Museum Road, TST. Take the Star Ferry to Tsim Sha Tsui, then take green minibus No 1 to the end of the line; open

Tues-Fri 1-9 p.m. Open Sat, Sun 10 a.m.-9 p.m. Phone for holiday hours. Admission $25 for adults, $15 for children. Features 500 exhibits, 60 percent of them hands-on.

Hong Kong Police Museum, 27 Coombe Road, Wanchai. Take China Motor Bus Number 15 from Exchange Square and exit near Stubbs and Peak crossroads; open 9 a.m.-5 p.m., except Tuesday, when it is open 2-5 p.m. Admission free. The history of the police force since 1844.

Lamma Island (Pg 14-15): Ferries leave from the Central terminals just west of the Star Ferry. Phone for hours and prices. Go to either village, Yung Shue Wan or Hung Shing Yeh, for their seafood restaurants.

Cheung Chau (Pg 14): Ferries leave from the Central terminals just west of the Star Ferry. Departures begin at 6:25 a.m. and continue throughout the day. $14 for adults, $7 for children. Scenic, gently sloping trails are ideal for small children and strollers.

Lantau Island (Pg 15): Ferries to Silvermine Bay leave from the Central terminals just west of Star Ferry. Departures begin at 6:25 a.m. and continue throughout the day. Cost for an ordinary ticket is $14 for adults, $7 for children. The Buddha and monastery are spectacular but the trip from Central can take two hours. Go on weekdays to avoid crowds. Lantau is hilly and the hiking trails are only suitable for older children, unless parents are able to carry them up steep hills.

Ocean Park (Pg 16): Take Citybus 629 at Star Ferry or Admiralty, about 15-20 minutes. The cost for the bus and admission is $150 for adults, $75 for children 3-11 years old. Admission without the bus is $130 for adults, $65 for children. Free admission for children under 3 and seniors over 60 (with a Hong Kong ID card). One adult can bring one child under 12 free. Family and Annual passes available. The park is open everyday of the year from 10 a.m. to 6 p.m. Admission price includes all rides, shows and exhibits. All shows run throughout the day. Phone for exact times.

Waterworld (Pg 17): Take Citybus 629 at Star Ferry or Admiralty. Bus, $11 for adults, $5.50 for children. Daytime entry is $60 for adults, $30 for children; night admission is $40 for adults, $20 for children. Season passes are $200 for adults, $150 for children. The park is open Jun 1-Sept 10 daily. In July and Aug, it is open 9 a.m.-9 p.m.. All other dates, it is open 10 a.m.-6.p.m.. It is also open weekends and public holidays from Sept 11-Oct 1.

Sai Kung Country Park (Pg 18): Ideal for picnics, this park features long beaches with crashing waves. As with all beaches in Hong Kong, care must be taken to observe shark warnings. Take MTR to Choi Hung station; Take green minibus No 1 to the village of Sai Kung.

New Territories (Pg 18): Take the MTR to Kowloon Tong and switch to the KCR (Kowloon China Railway). The train will take you to the Chinese border at Lo Wu and back in about 1 hour. A one-way ticket is $8, half price for children under 12, and free for children under 3.

Sung Dynasty Village (Pg 19): Lai Chi Kok, Kowloon. Take MTR to Mei Foo station, or take Bus 105 from West Point near Central. Open 10 a.m.-8 p.m. daily. Admission is $120 for adults, $85 for children under 12 on weekdays; $80 for adults, $35 for children on weekends. Children under 3 are free.